A Gambler's Little Instruction Book

John Gollehon

GOLLEHON BOOKS
GRAND RAPIDS, MICHIGAN

Library of Congress Catalog Card Number 94-72960

ISBN 0-914839-32-2
(International Standard Book Number)

GOLLEHON BOOKS are published by: Gollehon Press, Inc.,
6157 28th St. SE, Grand Rapids, MI 49546.
GOLLEHON BOOKS are available in quantity purchases;
contact Special Sales. Gollehon does not accept unsolicited
manuscripts. Brief book proposals are reviewed.

To Gamblers Everywhere...

1

The casino is crowded; you want to play but the tables are full. You've just spotted a guy ready to leave a table because he just lost all of his money.

But why would you want to take his place?

2

Winning should have no minimum or maximum limitations.

If you set a minimum limit on your winnings, I can almost assure you you'll end up a loser. You'll turn that modest win into a not-so-modest loss!

If you set a maximum limit on your winnings, I *can* assure you you'll never have the pleasure of counting chips in colors you've never seen before!

3

You might be surprised to know that a great many players don't even know what a win really is! They think a loss is really a win because they didn't lose *very much*. They're not satisfied with a win because they didn't win *enough*.

They are experts at turning winnings into losses.

4

Big egos and big losses go hand in hand.

5

If you don't have it with you, you can't lose it.

You might think this advice only applies to cash players. But understand that if you play on credit, like so many players do today, you *do* have it with you. Your entire credit line is in your back pocket.

So, if you decide to play on credit—although I don't recommend that you do—set your credit line as a loss limit, not as a status symbol to impress your friends.

6

Things to take with you:

Common sense
Discipline
Self-confidence
Instinct
Knowledge
And a *little* money

Things to leave at home:

Your ego
Anxiety
Systems
Greed
Desperation
Most of your money

7

Although you never want to set limits on your winnings, you must learn how to set limits on your losses. Set limits for each playing session, for each day, and for the trip. And stick to them!

Losses are inevitable. Knowing how to respond to a losing situation is just as important as knowing how to respond to a winning opportunity. In the first case, you put it in reverse; in the second case, you give it full throttle.

8

If you gamble with the attitude that you'll probably lose, you probably will.

9

Tell me all the reasons why you gamble, and I'll tell you all the reasons why you lose. Most players have all the wrong reasons. The *only* reason to gamble is to win!

⤳ 10 ⤳

Lady Luck is like a politician. She has such few favors to give, and too many friends to give them to.

11

"Far better it is to dare mighty things, to win glorious triumphs, even though checkered with failure, than to take rank with those poor spirits who neither enjoy much nor suffer much, because they live in the grey twilight that knows not victory nor defeat."

—Theodore Roosevelt

12

Casinos don't like to use the word "gambling" anymore. The euphemism of choice is "gaming."

But you're not there to play games. You're there to gamble, with all the inherent risks. Don't be fooled by the casino's little word game.

13

Casinos will entice you to "win" all the comps you can. But do you want to win comps, or do you want to win money?

14

If you think of a casino as your bank, you should know that the casino thinks of you the same way.

꩜ 15 ꩜

Good gambling is good timing.

It's one of my favorite little sayings, because it says so much in such few words. A good gambler doesn't rely on luck to pick the right time. A good gambler knows how to maximize his chances for "good timing," by minimizing all the times that aren't.

Think about it.

16

Chasing your losses is like chasing a wild goose.

If you've never met a wild goose before, it's probably because you got lost in the woods.

17

In the casino, everyone thinks they're an expert. An expert is a guy who knows 47 ways to make love, but can't find a girlfriend.

18

Why is it
you never see
anyone smiling
at a dice table?

19

Is there some reason why you work 40 hard hours to earn $500, then spend four hard hours giving it away to your favorite casino?

Has anyone, at any casino, ever thanked you?

⚬ 20 ⚬

Slot machines display your winnings on the credit meter in "credits," not dollars. The casino wants you to forget dollars and think credits. Credits are like points; but points have no value, and it's too easy for the unsuspecting player to think this way.

Don't let the casino mess with your mind.

21

Have you ever noticed that everyone in a casino seems to be in a hurry?

Are they in a hurry to win, or a hurry to lose?

22

If you like to watch people, watch them in a casino. They push other people around, they cuss, and they argue. They're having such a good time.

23

Playing in a casino with a friend is the best test of true friendship.

True friends want you to win.

True friends speak from their heart.

Have you ever wondered about some of your "friends"?

24

Many casinos today use buses to bring the players. Here's one of the most important rules of gambling:

When you see a bus full of players about to unload, get out of the way! These people have some serious losing to do. And they only have a few hours to do it!

25

There are so many casinos to visit today, scattered all over America. Which makes this rule of gambling all the more important:

Play only where you're comfortable, and only where you win. You'll soon learn that you're a lot more comfortable where you win. Or could it be that you win a lot more where you're comfortable?

Think about it.

26

It's hard
to win.
It's even
harder
to get even.

27

No one can win when their mind is cluttered with so many problems. Like in life, no one with a cluttered mind can make the right decisions. You must learn how to focus your concentration on one important matter at a time.

In the casino, there is only one important matter:

To Win!

28

Have you ever wondered why there are so many rude people in a casino?

Do you suppose it's because they're losing?

But some people can be rude even when they're winning.

Which can only mean they were losers before they walked in.

29

No one wants to be a loser. So learn how to be happy with a small win, because even a small win beats losing every time.

30

Over 95% of all players are not skilled, have no serious plan to win, and honestly anticipate a loss. Do you need another reason why 95% of all players lose?

31

Gambling is one of the most expensive forms of entertainment.

Why not trade a few of those "expensive" evenings for a nice gourmet dinner with your family.

32

The best way to counter the negative effects of a loss—and not just a gambling loss—is with a win. Do something that represents a win to you. Positive things tend to cancel out negative things.

33

In the casino,
you must have the
ability to recognize
an opportunity,
the wisdom to know
that you can't force
it to happen,
and the discipline to
quit when it's gone.

34

Greed is a loser's ally. Greed turns winners into losers.

35

Learn how to bet safely when you first begin a playing session to protect against sudden losses. Playing "catch-up" in the casino is an unenjoyable chore.

36

Don't change the value of money when you enter a casino. Does that twenty-dollar-bill look the same to you at Caesars as it does at McDonalds?

37

Wise gamblers increase their bets only when they're winning, and either decrease their bets or quit when they're losing. It's so simple, but it's probably the Number One trait of successful players.

ꕶ 38 ꕶ

Listen to your intuition. If you get the feeling it's a bad time to play, don't play. Successful people have learned how to respect their instincts.

It's been said that the most dangerous times to gamble are when you arrive and when you leave. To that I would like to add...
and all the time in between.

40

Temper your anxiety to gamble when you first arrive. Here's a suggestion: Before you leave home, schedule something else to do upon your arrival. Even something as simple as having lunch with your friends.

41

Don't confuse
"knowing how
to play"
with
"knowing how
to win."

42

Competitive people tend to be better gamblers. Are you competitive? Do you have the confidence to compete against a tougher foe?

If you think about it, it's what gambling is really all about.

43

Never bet against a trend.

If red came up ten times in a row, would you bet red again? Whether in sports, at the track, or at the tables, wise gamblers bet *with* the streak, never against it.

44

I can think of few things more dangerous than having credit in a casino.

45

Gambling experts always say you have to know the odds. Well, it's easy to know the odds. All you have to know is the odds are always against you.

46

Don't let someone else's play influence your own. If your friend is betting much more than you and winning, do you suppose that if you start betting a lot more you'll win, too?

Find your comfort level and stick with it.

Don't be suckered into making
"sucker" bets, unless, of course,
you don't know the difference,
in which case,
you're a sucker anyhow.

**Learn the smart bets
from the dumb bets
before you play.**

48

Anonymity is a precious thing. And I can think of no better place to have it than in a casino.

49

The longer you play, the more likely you will lose.

It's one of my favorite quotes that gambling writers preach and preach. Of course, it only applies to random games with a negative edge, like slots, roulette, keno, and dice. Skill games like blackjack and live poker, not to mention horse racing and sports betting, do not necessarily follow that premise. It is, however, a good reason to limit your play.

50

There is no such thing as "overdue."

How many times have you read that? You've read it in gambling books at least a zillion times because so many players can't get that notion out of their heads. If red came up ten times in a row, do you think that black is overdue? Please say, "No." And why isn't black overdue? Here's another thing you've read a zillion times: *The wheel has no memory.* Of course it doesn't. You know that, don't you? Please say, "Yes."

⚲ 51 ⚲

There is
no such thing as
"ready for a payoff."

Let me guess… you've read that at least a zillion times. If you're a slot player, how many times have you felt that way? Please tell me you've never felt that way. *Random games produce random results, independent of previous results.* Now it's been said a zillion and one times. "Overdue" and "ready for a payoff" are on top of the list of gambling misconceptions.

52

Casinos love players with betting systems. Does that tell you anything?

53

Learn how to hit and run. You win and you take your winnings home. Easy, isn't it? Easy if the casino just happens to close right after you win. But casinos don't close because players want to keep playing. It's called hit and *get* hit.

54

There are no systems
that work consistently.
But there are strategies.
And the best strategies
of all are at the blackjack
tables. There are two: a
basic strategy for player
options, and a powerful
strategy for keeping
track of played cards,
called card-counting.
Both work, but only if
you do.

55

All rich players don't
make big bets, and all
big bets don't come
from rich players.

56

Never make a bet you can't afford to lose.

This little gem has become trite. So many players rationalize their way around this gambling axiom that it has little meaning anymore.

The alert should sound *before* you gamble the rent money... *before* you gamble the money set aside for your kid's school clothes.

Gambling should be on the very bottom of your list of things to do with your money.

57

I have a friend who enjoys watching people gamble. And she can do this for hours. But what she really enjoys is watching people win. What a great lesson for all of us.

58

If you're a blackjack player, and you probably are, do you shop for the best table conditions, or do you just find a table and sit down?

I've always believed that this essential trait explains why women, for the most part, are better blackjack players than men.

They have the patience and the smarts to look for the best "buys."

59

Professional gamblers don't have it as easy as you think. There's a big difference between gambling because you have to, and gambling because you want to.

 60

Understand that no one builds $500 million casino/hotels in a break-even business. Casinos make money. Lots of money. To put it bluntly, these proud and pretentious mega-resorts are built on losers.

So, have you ever thought about investing in gambling stocks? If you can't beat 'em... buy 'em!

⟨ 61 ⟩

Don't be forced into playing at a table that requires a larger minimum bet than you want to make. You'll have to realize that casinos, like all other big corporations, are driven by the bottom line.

Just keep looking for that two-dollar table.

62

One of gambling's most famous quotes came from Nick The Greek, who said: "The most exciting thing is to win. The next most exciting thing is to lose."

We can all feel the goose bumps but don't you just wonder if maybe Nick had a little gambling problem?

63

Everyone has an aversion to being hustled. You want to guess how much hustling goes on in places like Las Vegas?

Dice dealers, for some reason, seem to be the most notorious, trying to hustle bets and tips from the players.

If it happens to you, you may use my standard line as you exit the table: "Where did you learn how to hustle, buddy, Ringling Brothers, or Barnum and Bailey?"

64

Always put some of your winnings aside to insure that you quit winners.

⤳ 65 ⤳

Never, never press a losing wager.

"Press" means to double the amount of your previous bet, in the hopes of recouping that loss and winning it back at the same time. Pressing a loss is one of the dumbest moves in gambling.

66

Be judicious in determining exactly how much money you want to risk the next time you plan a gambling trip. The money you take is your ammunition. The more ammunition you have, the better your chances of winning the battle, right?

Wrong! The more ammunition you have in your pocket, the better your chances of getting blown up!

One of my favorite examples of a dumb gambling tip comes from a pit boss:

"If you want to win thousands of dollars, you have to bet thousands of dollars."

Oh, the wisdom of a pit boss. Wouldn't you also think it's a great way to *lose* thousands of dollars?!

68

At the tables, you'll win some hands that you should have lost, and you'll lose some hands that you should have won. That's why they call it "gambling."

69

It always amazes me how so many people can pick the winning horse *after* the race.

70

Beware of False Prophets.

There are so many "guaranteed to win" gambling scams going on today, even published in reputable magazines and newspapers, that I must remind you: Don't let your dreams get in the way of your common sense.

71

After a nice win, an inexperienced player might tell you, "I'm safe because I'm betting with the casino's money."

No! It's a foolish notion to think you're holding the casino's money, as if to say the casino is just letting you keep it for a while. Which is probably what will happen.

When the chips are in your hands, the chips are *your* money!

72

The dice tables are a roller-coaster ride through the emotions, with winning and losing streaks that can jolt the teeth of inexperienced players. I love the game, but, then again, I love roller-coasters.

73

If you think you've gambled to the point where you might be getting addicted, get away from it, as far as you can, and completely forget about it. Find other things that can take the place of the "enjoyment" you looked forward to.

I've found that teaching a player with a gambling problem to "just bet a little" just doesn't work.

74

Gambling is fast becoming our national pastime, as state governors and legislators see it as easy taxes to collect. But now that the snowball is rolling, they also reason like a kid reasons: "If everyone else is doing it, why aren't *we* doing it?" These "kids" need a good scolding from their parents.

We all set limits on our gambling. Now it's time for gambling to set limits on itself.

75

All the best
strategies in
the world
won't help
you if you
aren't
disciplined.

ᘒ 76 ᘓ

Do more than just budget your money. Budget your time.

If you have the discipline to both limit your wagers and limit your sessions, you'll find a certain satisfaction in your play, win or lose, that can make you feel good about yourself. And that, my friend, is more important than winning, anyhow.

77

Just because you can afford to lose, don't use this lame excuse as a means of justifying a big loss. Sure, it might make it painless, but dropping your wallet down the sewer is painless, too. Or is it? Maybe a big loss won't bother you financially, but it can seriously affect your state of mind. Losing nags at everyone.

78

Easy spenders are easy losers.

The casino can outplay you even before you get there. Don't be tempted by the $2.99 steak-and-eggs breakfasts, and $4.99 buffets. You know and I know the $2.99 breakfast is going to cost you fifty bucks. To get there, you have to pass through the gantlet of beckoning dice dealers, rows and rows of blackjack tables, and probably the lowest paying slot machines in town.

ᦈ 80 ᦈ

Let each losing session serve a purpose. Learn from it; don't simply let it pass. If you analyze the session, you'll find something *not* to do the next time.

81

This is a tough rule for a gambler to live by, but try to understand that every gambling session must end.

When you say, "One more roll," or "One more shoe," stick to it.

It's especially tough when you're on the last day of your trip, and you know it might be several months or even a year before you play again.

Smile when you've played your last hand, shrug your shoulders when you've pulled the handle for the last time.

There will always be another opportunity to look forward to.

82

The wise gambler
knows how
to enjoy a
football game
without
betting it.

83

Pay little attention to what your friends tell you to do.

The chances are your friends are full of superstitions and misconceptions.

Get yourself a good book. Which book? That's like asking a Chevy dealer which Ford to buy. (My list is in the front of this book.)

84

Gambling mirrors life in so many different ways. We all take risks to benefit from the rewards. We all take risks because we know we can learn from them. We all take risks because they challenge us to succeed. In life, we can control these risks. In the casino, they are stacked against us. Don't draw the analogy too closely.

85

A winner is someone who knows how to deal with losing. A loser is someone who doesn't.

86

You can always identify inexperienced players because they are so indecisive. Basically, they're guessing.

You can always identify knowledgeable gamblers because they know exactly what to do. Basically, they're making "educated" guesses.

It doesn't mean they're always going to win, it just means they have less likelihood of guessing wrong.

87

Sports bettors and horseplayers are notorious for using systems to pick winners. The problem is that anyone can create a system that worked in the past. But no one can assure you it will work in the future.

88

The only systems that work are the systems that work on your own gullibility. Keep repeating to yourself:

"There are no systems. There are no systems."

89

Knowledge is power. But the casino knows more than you do.

Knowledge is also protection. And the best knowledge of all is knowing that you can always walk out the door.

⤳ 90 ⤳

If you have a fear of gambling, it almost always reflects a fear of yourself. A fear that you might get carried away, that you might lose control.

If you don't have the confidence in yourself to put away that fear, either find the self-control to restore your confidence or stop gambling.

Your fear is trying to tell you something.

91

The real value of winning is not what you're going to buy with your winnings, but that you won.

If you were so fortunate to win, give some of your winnings to other players who are down on their luck.

At the slots, put some coins in their tray. At the tables, make a bet for them as you leave. By doing this, you'll have turned your winnings into even greater winnings.

93

If you win, and you're not excited, then you haven't won at all. Maybe you think you have to win a lot of money to get excited. But that's not what winning is. Winning is a state of mind. So is losing. And I have yet to see an excited loser.

94

A gambler who doesn't have the patience to wait will have nothing to wait for.

95

You would think that casino owners, paranoid as they are, would feel that proverbial pea under their pillow, knowing that someone's always out there trying to find a way to beat them.

Fact is: They all get a good night's sleep.

○ 96 ○

I have a friend who plays blackjack to relax and enjoy himself.

Slow players don't bother him. Inexperienced players making all the wrong moves don't bother him. Even a rude dealer doesn't phase him. He's oblivious to it all.

And wouldn't you know it, he wins often. But he's a winner whether he wins or loses.

Don't let anyone ruin your fun when gambling. More importantly, don't ruin it yourself.

98

After a football game that you watched, consider your response to someone who asks, "How did your team do?"

If you like the winning team, your answer is "They won."

If it's your favorite team or alma mater, your answer is "We won."

If you had a bet on the winning team, your answer is "I won."

◎ 99 ◎

I firmly believe that what separates winners from losers is much more than luck, and even much more than skill. It's an uncanny ability to just know when. When to jump on it, when to ease back, and when to walk.

☽ 100 ☾

When you've acquired the discipline to actually walk around the casino with chips in your hand, and to resist playing (it's a test I recommend everyone take) you'll feel good that you have control over *it*. It doesn't have control over *you*.

101

A good gambler knows how to quit winners. A better gambler knows how to quit losers.

ᥫ 102 ᥫ

Winning in the short term is easy.
You win, you count your money,
you quit for life. But who does that?

Winning in the long term is a little
tougher. You lose, you count your
losses, you quit until the next time.
But by the time the next time comes,
you will have forgotten about how
much you lost the last time. And the
time before that. It's called rolling
back the odometer. When the time
comes for another gambling binge,
you set the meter back to zero. If
only you knew how many miles
were on that old clunker.

103

I find it strange that "professional" blackjack players get all the attention. It's funny because the only gamblers I know who deserve that attention are horseplayers, sports bettors, or poker players. But of the ones I know, few others know, and my guess is they want to keep it that way.

104

Don't confuse "instinct" with "superstition." When I gamble, I take along my most trusted friend; I never gamble with a fool.

⚮ 105 ⚮

Don't confuse "greed" with "aggression."
An aggressive player will set no limits on his winnings.
A greedy player will have no winnings to worry about.

✑ 106 ✑

Definition of a greedy player: One who bets back all of his winnings, trying to force more wins. Greedy players can be considered self-destructive.

107

Definition of an aggressive player: One who knows how to take advantage of a winning opportunity, by not being afraid to bet at justifiably higher levels. Aggressive players have a "killer" instinct. The wise gambler knows this difference well. Greedy players take unnecessary risks. Aggressive players are cunning and patient. They know when to strike; and they strike hard.

୨ 108 ଓ

Be wary of comps. They come with an assortment of pitfalls, not the least of which is the tendency to want to play only where you're getting the comps, to play for more hours than you want to, and to bet at a higher average level than you want to.

The wise gambler varies his betting levels as the conditions change. But the comped player feels a certain "pressure" to keep his betting levels unusually high. Don't let the casino control the way you play.

109

Another way comps can destroy a player is by reducing—if not entirely removing—the adversarial relationship between player and casino. Comped players tend to think of the casino as their "friend." The casino wants your money. You want the casino's money. Does this sound like a "friendly" encounter?

110

You can beat the odds, but you can't beat the percentages.

111

Good gamblers are like good agents. They can be vicious.

ᥫ 112 ᥫ

Don't get the idea you can make a living at the dice tables, or even the blackjack tables. Unless your idea of living is a cardboard box under the overpass.

❂ 113 ❂

Some people will tell you that gambling per se is a bad habit. But for many gamblers, it's not gambling that's bad, it's the *way* they gamble.

∽ 114 ∾

Casinos don't use chips for convenience; they use chips to help blur the images of our valued friends: Mr. Jackson, Mr. Grant, and Mr. Franklin. With plastic chips to play with, our money values get a little fuzzy. But it all returns to sharp focus when we get home.

⤶ 115 ⤷

Don't let other players influence the way you bet. Learn how to tune out other players and all other distractions. You must learn how to be in complete control of your game plan.

Here's how John Alcamo makes the point in *Atlantic City Behind The Tables*:

(Quoting a pit boss) We once had five baccarat players from Brazil betting $50,000 a hand. Halfway through the shoe one of our regular customers sat down to play. Two hands later he left. He said his $500 bets made him feel cheap!

) 116 (

The most
important thing
a gambler can do
is not to win,
but not to lose.

☾ 117 ☾

The term "grinding it out" can have different meanings. It depends on who's doing the "grinding."

Is the casino grinding *you* out, or are *you* grinding out a profit?

It's the mark of a good player who can hold his own while he watches other players come and go. A better term for it is "Staying Power." It increases your chances of catching that proverbial "hot hand."

ᏮᏏ 118 Ꮯ

Gambling should be a planned "destination" trip. Never go gambling on a whim.

ℭ 119 ℭ

The true mark of a tough player is a conservative betting strategy to open play. As play continues, your bets will depend on your successes, or failures. If you falter, your losses will have been minimized. If you're catching a good hand, your bets will increase as your winnings increase. It really isn't that complicated.

৩ 120 ৫

One of my favorite quotes comes from a dice dealer:

"The toughest part of this game is to bet heavy when the dice are passing. Most players don't bet enough during a hot streak."

Of course, this great advice applies to any gambling endeavor. How many times have you experienced a winning opportunity and didn't take full advantage?

ͽ 121 ͼ

You aren't aggressive enough if
you don't feel it in your shoes,
like two Titan booster rockets;
you don't even think about
the chance encounter with
five-hundred-dollar chips
piling up in front of you.

If you do think about it,
you probably think only of
its remoteness.

Other Great Gambling Titles From Gollehon Books

Las Vegas Behind The Tables

Las Vegas Behind The Tables Part 2

Atlantic City Behind The Tables

Lifestyles Of A High Roller

Slot Machine Mania

Video Poker Mania

Winner Take All

Beat The Track

Casino Games

Off The Strip